Horses
up Close

Christopher Blazeman

Consultant

Timothy Rasinski, Ph.D.
Kent State University

Publishing Credits

Dona Herweck Rice, *Editor-in-Chief*
Robin Erickson, *Production Director*
Lee Aucoin, *Creative Director*
Conni Medina, M.A.Ed., *Editorial Director*
Jamey Acosta, *Editor*
Stephanie Reid, *Photo Editor*
Rachelle Cracchiolo, M.S.Ed., *Publisher*

Image Credits

Cover & p.1 E. Spek/Dreamstime; p.3 Alexia Khruscheva/Shutterstock; p.4–5 Alexia Khruscheva/Shutterstock; p.6 Mary Morgan/iStockphoto; p.7 Julia Remezova/Shutterstock; p.8 Tim Platt/Getty Images; p.9 top: Margo Harrison/Shutterstock; p.9 bottom: Pirita/Shutterstock; p.10 top: Mariait/Shutterstock; p.10 bottom: RonTech2000/iStockphoto; p.10 Schweinpriester/Shutterstock; p10 Agata Dorobek/Shutterstock; p.11 left: Patryk Kosmider/Shutterstock; p.11 right: Erik Lam/Shutterstock; p.12 top: Cindy Singleton/iStockphoto; p.12 bottom: JUAN SILVA/iStockphoto; p.13 AFP/Getty Images/Newscom; p.14 Cynoclub/Shutterstock; p.15 Andreas Meyer/Shutterstock; p.16 Schweinepriester/Shutterstock; p.16 Zuzule/Shutterstock; p.17 top: Paul Maguire/Shutterstock; p.17 bottom: Karel Gallas/Shutterstock; p.18 top: Lucian Coman/Dreamstime; p.18 bottom: 1000 Words/Shutterstock; p.19 Auremar/Shutterstock; p.20 Abramova Kseniya/Shutterstock; p.21 Rita Januskeviciute/Shutterstock; p.22 left: Jaquez/Shutterstock; p.22 right: Dee Hunter/Shutterstock; p.23 top: Eric Hood/iStockphoto; p.23 bottom: Marekuliasz/Shutterstock; p.24 left: David Burrows/Shutterstock; p.24 Tomas Hajek/Dreamstime; p.25 top: Margo Harrison/Shutterstock; p.25 bottom: Burbank, E.A. (Elbridge Ayer); p.26 top: Alexandru Magurean/iStockphoto; p.26 bottom: Jim Parkin/Shutterstock; p.27 Groomee/Shutterstock

Based on writing from *TIME For Kids*.

TIME For Kids and the *TIME For Kids* logo are registered trademarks of TIME Inc. Used under license.

Teacher Created Materials

5301 Oceanus Drive
Huntington Beach, CA 92649-1030
http://www.tcmpub.com

ISBN 978-1-4333-3617-1

© 2012 Teacher Created Materials, Inc.

Printed in Malaysia
Thumbprints.24449

Table of Contents

If You Were a Horse

Have you ever wished you were a horse?

If you were a horse, you would run like the wind.

You would have a long tail and **mane**.

You would be powerful and strong.

Oh, how wonderful to be a horse!

All About Horses

Horses are beautiful animals with strong muscles. A horse can easily carry a person on its back.

A horse's powerful legs help the animal run far and jump high. Some horses can run more than 50 miles per hour!

Horses are fast, too. They are one of the fastest animals in the world. People like to watch horse races and guess which horse will run the fastest.

Horses come in many colors. They can be black, white, brown, gray, red, yellow, and more. Sometimes they are two or three colors at once.

A white spot at a horse's eye level or above is called a star. Any white mark below its eyes but above its nostrils is called a stripe.

Did you know that a zebra is a type of horse?

Some horses have spots. Some horses have stripes. Some have both, and some have none.

Horses can be tall or short. Many horses are taller than people, but some horses are very small.

Some miniature (MIN-ee-uh-chur)
horses are trained to help blind people.
They are like seeing-eye dogs.

A miniature horse may be
only two feet tall!

No matter their size, all horses have the same body parts. They are called points. Here are some of a horse's points.

muzzle

A horse has only one toe on each foot. Each toe is covered by a horny **hoof**. A horseshoe is used to protect the hoof.

ear

mane

A **muzzle** is a horse's jaw and nose. The **withers** are the ridge between a horse's two shoulder bones.

withers

tail

How Horses Live

Horses live all over the world. In the wild, they live on plains.

With people, they may live
in fields, stables, and corrals.

Since they are so active,
horses are big eaters. They eat
plants.

They especially like grasses and grains and sweet treats like apples and sugar cubes.

There are seven million horses in the United States.

A **stallion** is a male horse. A female is a **mare**. Boy horse babies are called colts. Girl horse babies are called fillies. All horse babies are called **foals**.

A mare nurses her foal to feed it. She keeps her foal near her while it is growing.

A mare also protects her foal. If there is danger, she will kick or bite anything that may harm her baby.

A horse's eyes are on the side of its head. Because of this, a horse can see almost everywhere around itself without turning its head. It can also see two different things at once because each eye sees something different.

One thing a horse cannot see is whatever is right in front of its head! So, a horse can't see the food it eats.

Horses have been helping people for thousands of years. They make people's lives easier by doing the hard jobs.

The Nez Perce Indians were once the best horse riders and breeders in the United States.

Nez Perce chief

Some horses pull wagons and farm machinery. Some work for the police. Some work in the circus. Some help cowboys ride the range.

Throughout time, people have needed horses to help them.

Many people say that dogs
are people's best friends. But
horses may be even more
important.

foal

hoof

mane

mare

muzzle

stallion

withers